Beginning Guitar

By Artie Traum.

Beginning Guitar

By Artie Traum.

Exclusive Distributors
Music Sales Corporation
257 Park Avenue South, New York, NY 10010 USA
Music Sales Limited
8/9 Frith Street, London W1V 5TZ England
Music Sales Pty. Limited
120 Rothschild Street, Rosebery, Sydney, NSW 2018, Australia

Order No. AM 36997
US ISBN 0.8256.2333.2
UK ISBN 0.7119.0807.9

Book design by Nina Clayton
Cover design by Alison Fenton
Cover photography by Robert Hansen-St urm
Modelled by Artie Traum
Edited by Amy Appleby and Peter Pickow

Printed in the United States of America by
Vicks Lithograph and Printing Corporation

Amsco Publications
New York/London/Sydney

This book is dedicated to my first teachers: Happy Traum, Mark Silber (the world's greatest fingerpicker), Rory Block (who learned the secrets of country blues by age fourteen), Doc Watson (for my favorite flatpicking records), and other friends who were kind enough to share their knowledge of the guitar with me.

CONTENTS

INTRODUCTION

I don't think I'll ever forget the feeling I had the day I bought my first guitar. I bought it from an old Greek gentleman who collected and traded guitars from his tiny apartment in New York's Greenwich Village. I picked out an ancient Washburn guitar, built around 1910. That guitar would be considered quite a collector's item nowadays, but that didn't matter to me then.

I left his little shop walking on a cloud, the guitar clutched firmly in my hand. But on the way home I stopped dead in my tracks. A cold sweat came over me. I owned the guitar. Now what would I do? I didn't have the slightest idea. I couldn't tune it, make chords, strum it, or use a pick. I had just spent my last dollar—with one subway token left in my pocket—for a guitar I knew nothing about.

I only knew one thing for sure. I loved guitars. And I loved guitar music—from folk and blues to rock and classical. Any guitar music was all right with me. I had grown up on the tight rockabilly strumming of the Everly Brothers, had gone to high school listening to Chet Atkins, had taken my first driving lesson with Eric Clapton on the radio, and had studied for finals with the classical sounds of Julian Bream on my stereo. I knew I wanted to play. I wanted to play so badly I could taste it . . . feel it. But where to start?

There's an old joke that goes: "Excuse me, can you tell me how to get to Carnegie Hall?" The answer: "Practice!" It's a corny joke, but somehow it stuck in my mind the day I bought my guitar. I went home and glanced at a bunch of chord diagrams a friend had written out for me. I carefully began to follow his instructions, stretching the fingers of my left hand across the strings on the fingerboard. It seemed to take forever, but after a while I had figured out an E chord. Triumph! A small step for mankind! Yet when I strummed across the strings with my right hand, I was in for a rude shock. The sound that came out was a cross between a rooster crowing and fingernails scratching across a blackboard. If it took this long to make one simple chord, I thought, it might take an eternity to play well. I called my friend in a state of panic. He had been playing for about six months, but he answered my questions like an expert.

"You have to be patient," he said. "Rome wasn't built in a day!"

"But how long did it take Jimi Hendrix to learn?" I asked.

"It doesn't matter," he replied coolly, "you're not Hendrix!"

Undaunted, I decided to try the guitar again. In a few hours I had learned three basic chords, shaky though they were. I was on my way. The only problem was that my fingers were very, very sore.

"What did you expect," my friend asked, "that the guitar would play itself?"

So, with sore fingers, a great deal of confusion, and some degree of frustration, I continued to chip away at the mysteries of my guitar. Am I ever glad that I did. The instrument literally changed my life. It has brought me more pleasure, more satisfaction, and more pure joy than anything else in my life—with the possible exception of chocolate.

Looking back, I recall the feeling I had when I first tried to make chords, strum, or use a flatpick. Each small victory seemed to enrich my life in ways I'd never dreamed possible. That's why I am happy to pass on some of the things I've learned to you. I hope this book will be helpful—and fun to use. I know that it all seems like a big mystery to you now—but keep on pickin', I promise the effort will be worth it.

Oh, by the way, when it comes to playing guitar, all of us are, in a way, beginners. I have been playing for twenty-five years and I still find many new techniques and musical ideas waiting to be explored. I'm sure that all professional guiarists—from George Benson to Andrés Segovia—would say the same thing: There is always something more to be discovered about the guitar!

Practicing

"A word about practicing. Don't practice twelve hours a day or anything like that. You'll just wear yourself out. Play for a while, until you get tired, and then put it down. Always make sure you are enjoying yourself. . . ."

Clarence 'Gatemouth' Brown—Blues Guitarist

Of course, you are going to have to practice. There is no getting around that. But what kind of practicing will you do? That is a very simple question, but don't underestimate its importance.

I was brought up to believe that in order to get anywhere in life, you had to work like a maniac. Perhaps that is true in business, or in the military, or in the academic world. But with music, it is another matter.

Guitar playing should be fun. It should never feel like work. If your hands don't tingle just a little before you pick up the guitar, if you don't feel a slight ticklish feeling before you practice—don't bother. Other teachers may tell you otherwise; I can't say they are wrong. But this is how I feel.

I'll never forget how much I hated practicing the piano when I was a little kid. My parents had convinced me to take lessons, but I really didn't want to. I never learned a thing, and to this day, I can barely play. On the other hand, I learned to play the guitar virtually overnight. You know why? I *wanted* to play . . . and I played *what* I wanted *when* I wanted. It just so happened that I wanted to play all of the time! I played my guitar when I should have been doing homework, when I would have been running errands, and when I should have been asleep. I hardly ever put the darn thing down.

Rick Nielson of the rock band Cheap Trick once said, "If you can't have fun with what you're doing, you really shouldn't do it." Of course, there will have to be a certain amount of *effort* if you are going to get anywhere with your guitar. But the bottom line is enjoyment. Go at your own pace, relax, and enjoy yourself.

Holding the Guitar

You've just gotten you new guitar home and you've opened the case. The guitar is staring at you, asking to be played. You reach down, grab the strings, and start to pull the guitar toward you.

"Not that way, you klutz!" the guitar screams, strings clanging discordantly. "Pick me up where the neck meets the body . . . gently."

You try again, pulling it out of the case.

"That's better," the guitar sighs. "Now put me on your lap."

"This is rather sudden," you say, stunned. "I've only just met you!"

Although later you will probably want to play guitar standing up, for now you will find it much easier to learn and practice if you sit on a nice, hard, straightback chair and hold the guitar as in the picture below. When you can play as well as Elvis (Presley or Costello) you may hang your guitar around your neck with a strap and even tapdance while you play.

Once you are seated comfortably, you will be looking down at the guitar from above. From this bird's-eye view, you will see the basic parts of your guitar. Off to your left, at the end, you will find the *peghead* with the *tuning pegs* attached. Attached to the tuning pegs are *strings* which run all the way along the *neck* to the *bridge* of your guitar. You will have to reach over and adjust the tuning pegs to tune your guitar. An out-of-tune guitar is basically worthless, and many a guitarist has been tempted to trade in or smash a guitar that won't tune properly.

The string closest to you is called the low E-string. It is the thickest string. Guitarists generally start tuning with this string—although you may want to start with another string once you are familiar with the tuning process.

"Okay, Mr. Segovia," the guitar taunts. "Let's see if you are clever enough to get me in tune."

Tuning

Bluegrass guitarists like to joke that "you can tune a guitar, but you can't tuna fish." That's certainly true. When it comes to guitar, there are several ways to tune, all of which have their advantages. As you can see, there are six strings on your instrument. They are named as follows:

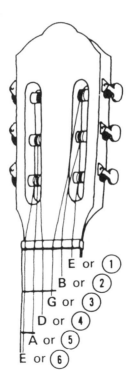

E or ①
B or ②
G or ③
D or ④
A or ⑤
E or ⑥

One way to tune is to play a note on the piano and then try to match the sound by turning the tuning peg until the string is properly taut. Here are the notes on the piano that correspond to each string of your guitar.

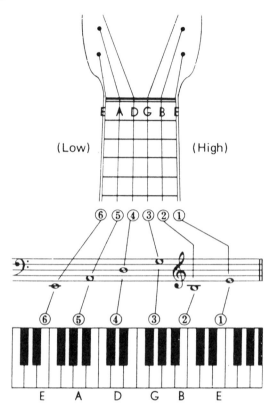

This method is good because after a while you will train your ear to hear the subtle differences between notes in tune and those that are out of tune.

You may use a *tuning fork* to get a true A note—which, of course, corresponds to the fifth string of your guitar. Once your A string is in tune, you may use it as a reference to get the other strings in tune. The standard tuning setup of the strings on your guitar makes this an easy matter; just follow this procedure: Fret (press down) the sixth string at the 5th fret and you will get an A note. That should correspond to the sound of the open fifth string—which is already in tune. If it does not, the sixth string must be adjusted. Likewise, the fifth string at the 5th fret should equal the fourth (D) string; the fourth string at the 5th fret should equal the third (G) string, and the second string at the 5th fret should equal the first (E) string.

The third string, however, must be fretted at the 4th fret in order to equal the second (B) string. Many guitarists use this method to check their tuning when they suspect a string has gone flat (too low) or sharp (too high).

The *electronic tuning device* is one of the great inventions of modern times. It can make tuning very easy and help your ear to develop at the same time. I would recommend investing in a tuner for three good reasons: First, when you are out of tune, the tuner will tell you precisely which string (or strings) is out. Second; the tuner makes it extremely easy to get in tune with other musicians by giving a standard reference point. Third; it makes it possible to tune in noisy surroundings because you don't have to actually hear the notes—the machine indicates pitch visually. This is why you will see rock guitarists using tuners on stage where the background noise makes it impossible to tune by ear.

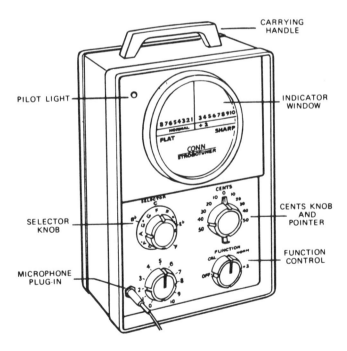

Never underestimate the importance of being in tune. As hit songwriter/guitarist Livingston Taylor once told me: "A guitarist must be perfectly in tune. There is literally no excuse in this day and age to be out of tune. A guitar in tune is a happy guitar!"

Strings

Your guitar may come with *steel* or *nylon* strings, depending on the style of guitar you have bought. Nylon strings are generally used in classical music, although jazz players like Charlie Byrd and Earl Klugh employ nylon strings for their fingerstyle techniques. Some folk guitarists use nylon strings as well. Nylon strings are good for beginners because they are easier on the fingers than steel strings.

Steel strings are generally used in country music, rock and roll, and folk music because of their twangy resonance and versatility. Light gauge strings are recommended for beginners, particularly when using steel strings. There are also very light *silk and steel* strings available that combine nylon and steel effectively. I have used these strings for quite some time and find that they sound bright and clear, and are easy on the fingers.

When choosing your strings, keep in mind that the differences between brands are slight. In fact, more expensive strings are not necessarily the best. I suggest you experiment with different types and gauges before settling on any specific type of string.

Your strings will have to be kept in good shape as you continue to play. Most professional guitarists change their strings quite often.

"My hands sweat like crazy," country-folk guitar whiz David Bromberg once told me, "so I change my strings after every show. They go *dead* (lose their bright sound) very quickly, so I have no choice."

David Bromberg's case may be a little bit extreme, but strings do wear out, or get rusty. I suggest wiping them off with a clean cloth after practicing.

Sore Fingers

Your fingers will get sore. I can guarantee that. The more you practice and play, the more they will hurt—up to a point. It is simple biology. Your soft fingertips, pressing against the thin wires of the guitar, will become somewhat sore. But don't worry. The discomfort is only temporary. It *will* go away. After a while, you will develop callouses on your fingers and it won't hurt to play.

In the meantime, there is little you can do to get around soreness. Clarence 'Gatemouth' Brown, the Grammy Award–winning guitarist from New Orleans, suggests soaking your fingers in vinegar before you play. He also recommends rubbing the juice of the aloe vera plant on your fingertips after playing. "That will take away the soreness," he claims.

CHORDS

Let's put aside further technical talk about guitars until later and get down to some playing. We'll start by looking at a diagram of the fingerboard.

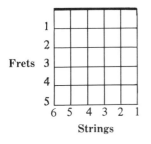

As you can see, this diagram represents a straight-on view of the fingerboard. Each string has a number, as you can see under the chart. The frets are also numbered, beginning with the fret closest to the nut (represented by the thick line on top).

Of course you will be using your left hand to play notes and chords, so we will need numbers for your fingers as well.

A note is a single string played by itself. It may be the third string, or the fifth—and it may be fretted by pressing down with a finger of your left hand, somewhere along the neck. Let's try to fret the fourth string (called the D string) at the 2nd fret, using the first finger of the left hand. On the diagram it looks like this:

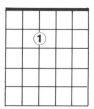

Now, let's hold that note and add two others below it, both at the 2nd fret.

A

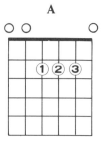

This is an A chord. Now, with your right hand, brush down across the strings near the sound hole. Can you hear all of the notes? Are they ringing clearly? Or is it a muffled mess? If it sounds jumbled, you must adjust your fingers so they press down correctly.

Let me give you a few pointers on how to hold your left hand so that the chord rings out properly. Place your thumb on the back of the guitar neck, to give your hand strength and leverage.

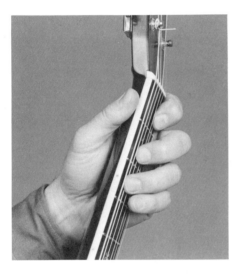

Now, make sure your fingers are pressing the strings very close to the fret, without actually being on the fret. You shouldn't have to push too hard, but give it enough power so that the notes are clear. If your sound is muted you probably need to exert more pressure. By the way, the nails on your left hand should be cut relatively short to prevent them from interfering with clear tones.

Your right hand, for now, should simply curl up slightly and strum down lightly across the strings. We'll get into more complicated strumming soon, but for now just brush down.

As an alternative stroke, you might want to slide across the string with the fleshy part of your thumb, hitting one string at a time. Your right thumb will play a very important part in your playing later—particularly if you play fingerstyle folk music or jazz.

So, let's try the A chord one more time, before moving on to our second chord, the E chord. The E chord is one of the richest first-position chords you will learn, and you will probably find yourself reaching for an E chord time and time again. It looks like this:

Try strumming across the E chord. The clue to playing guitar lies in your ability to change chords at will. Try going back and forth from the A chord to the E chord. Here is how this simple chord progression looks in rhythmic notation:

Each slash (✐) represents one beat in a four-beat measure of music. So every time you see the slash, give it one downward strum. Do this until you can change chords easily and cleanly without losing the beat.

There is one more thing I must mention. When you play an A chord, try to stay away from the low E-string. At times it will sound fine with an A chord, but it may also sound dissonant or harsh to the ear. You will certainly hear this as you play.

John Henry

Now you are ready for your first song. I thought I'd start with a bluesy folk song called "John Henry" because it has always been one of my favorites. I've always had a deep love for the blues, and while this song is not strictly a *blues*, it certainly has a blues feel to it. You can play "John Henry" using the two chords we have just learned, and most of the time you will simply stay with the A chord.

When it comes to changing chords, my good friend Pat Alger likes to talk about economy of motion. "Move your hands as little as possible," he tells students at guitar workshops, "and don't overshoot your mark." This is excellent advice. The movement back and forth from A to E should be easy and fluent, and you should use as little energy as possible.

John Henry

Your strumming hand should also move as little as possible. Many eager beginning guitarists flail the strings as though they were making an overhand smash in a tennis match. The sound produced is a nerve-jangling vibration of strings—like being in the wrong gear in a sports car. Your touch—the way your fingers hit the strings, the tone you produce, and the ease with which you play—will be very important later on. It's best to start correctly and play with a light, but firm touch.

Picking the Strings

Now that you know two chords—and the song "John Henry"—let's move on to some right-hand technique, known as picking or fingerpicking. There are many ways to approach fingerstyles with your right hand; from the country-folk picking made popular by Merle Travis and Chet Atkins, to the jazz-flavored styles of Earl Klugh and Charlie Byrd. Classical players also rely on a fluid right-hand style, so whatever your preference, you will have to learn fingerpicking to some extent.

I believe that right-hand technique begins and ends with the thumb. In fact, when a guitarist tells me he or she is all thumbs, I consider that good news. Your thumb should set the basic rhythm for any song you are playing, eventually bouncing from string to string on the bass notes.

Let's begin with your thumb plucking the fifth string while you fret an A chord. The fifth string is an A, so it is the *root* note of the chord. Lightly pluck down on the fifth string with your thumb, following with a brush downward across the other strings with your index finger, or the curled fingers of your right hand.

What you want to do is play a bass note with your thumb, then brush down . . . play another bass note, brush down again . . . bass note, brush down . . . etc. Rhythmically, it should look like this.

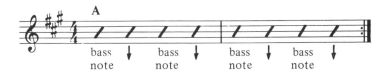

When you play this strum, try to sound like a smooth, Nashville-style, country-music picker. Take it slowly at first, gradually increasing the tempo.

Now try the same strum on an E chord. This time, hit the E (or sixth) string in the bass, to correspond with the *root* note of chord.

Once you have this basic strum down, you might try the alternating bass, that is, alternating between the fifth and sixth strings with your thumb.

Now try "John Henry" with a full strum. It should start sounding richer and fuller right away. We will come back to this strumming technique later, but now let's take a look at the third chord in the key of A, the D chord:

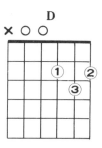

Now that you know the A, E, and D chords in the key of A, you will be able to play a wide variety of songs. In fact, most country-western, folk, and rock and roll songs use only three chords! Let's try a very well-known traditional song, "Will the Circle Be Unbroken." This tune has been played and recorded by scores of performers over the years. (Probably the most famous version is the title cut on the Nitty Gritty Dirt Band's best-selling album.)

Will the Circle Be Unbroken

Once you can handle the chord changes easily and smoothly, try playing "Will the Circle Be Unbroken" with the alternating-bass strum you have just learned. Here's how it looks:

Will the Circle Be Unbroken

To Pick or Not to Pick: Flatpicks, Fingerpicks, and Thumbpicks

Many guitarists find that fingerpicks produce a crisper, brighter sound on their guitar, particularly with steel-string models. While this is certainly true, I would not recommend using them at this time, although you might want to get a set of them to see how they work. I used fingerpicks for many years, eventually discarding them so I could *feel* the strings with my fingertips and nails. This is an important consideration for the beginning guitarist, who will need his or her sense of touch to get rooted with the instrument.

Flatpicks are another story. They are generally made of plastic, although in the old days, guitarists loved the natural resilience of tortoise-shell picks. These turtles are now an endangered species, so don't bother looking for tortoise-shell picks these days. You should choose a few different flatpicks to fool around with. They are very inexpensive, which is good since they often get lost.

Picks come in hard, medium, and soft gauges. Buy one of each and see which feels best in your hands. I began playing with a very soft pick, since its pliability seemed to make playing easier for me. Eventually, I switched to hard picks because they produce a brighter, more rounded tone. It is simply a matter of personal choice.

Whether to use fingerpicks, flatpicks, or no picks at all, is a decision only you can make. Earl Klugh, an innovative jazz-style guitarist, does not use fingerpicks (although he has used a thumbpick) on his nylon-string guitar. Albert King, the legendary blues guitarist, plays everything with his bare thumb, still managing to get a percussive sound. Freddie King, on the other hand, uses a thumbpick and one fingerpick to alternate between strings. Andrés Segovia, of course, uses no picks for his classical playing. Eric Clapton, who plays many styles of guitar, generally uses a medium-gauge flatpick on his electric.

There is an incredible range of approaches to guitar playing. Some styles are more conducive to the use of picks. You'd be hard-pressed to find a bluegrass rhythm-guitarist without a flatpick in his or her

hand. And most electric jazz-players use a flatpick
as well. The legendary jazz guitarist Wes
Montgomery once said that he developed his incredibly flexible thumb-style because "no one told me *not*
to do it! I made my own way!" Eventually, you will
have to make that choice for yourself. Like an ab-
stract painter, you should learn the basics before
making your own moves.

Now, let's return to "Will the Circle Be Unbroken"
and play it using a flatpick. Hold the pick between
your right thumb and index finger—not too tight,
but not too loose either. You want to exert a fair
amount of pressure without overdoing it.

As you can see, only a small part of the pick should
project beyond the edges of your thumb and finger.
Your wrist should stay relaxed—to get the feeling,
shake the pick as if you were shaking a
thermometer.

Now, hit the fifth string while holding an A chord
and strum down as you did before. Is the sound
clean? Can you hear all of the notes? If the sound is
muddy, don't despair. Pete Seeger once said that
"playing guitar is as easy as walking—but it took us
all a couple of years to learn how to walk!" You will
get the hang of the pick eventually, if you keep at
it.

Midnight Special

Here's another very popular folk song to try in the key of A. Notice that one chord is different. Instead of an E chord, we are going to use an E7 chord in this progression.

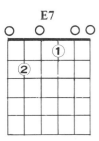

Midnight Special

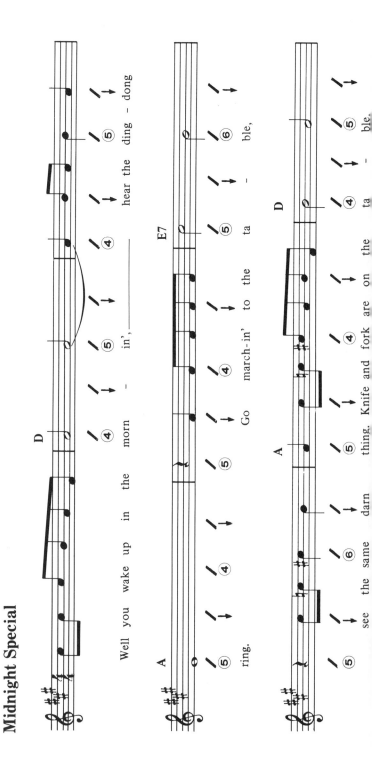

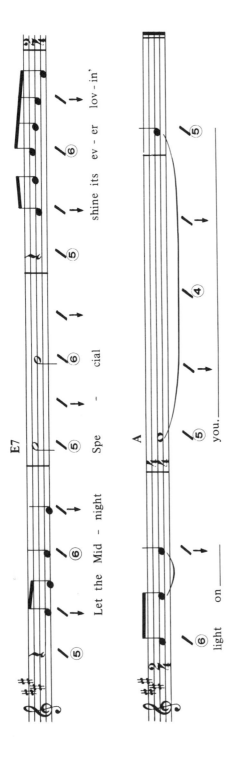

Chord Study

Now that you have learned the basic chords in the key of A, let's take a look at some other chords. Many chords overlap from one key to another. The D and A chords, for example, are equally at home in the key of D and the key of A, and they show up in other keys as well. Let's look at three chords in the key of D:

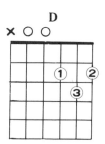

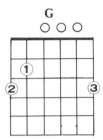

Now let's try a version of "Midnight Special" in the key of D.

Midnight Special

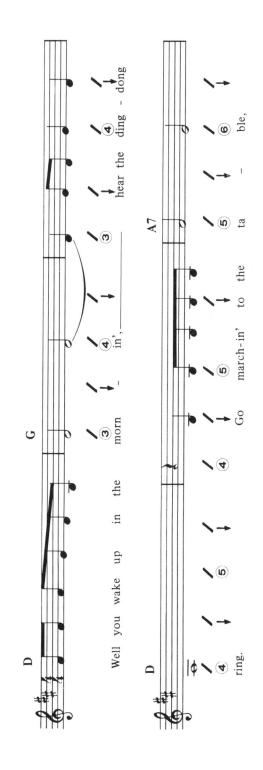

Well you wake up in the morn - in', hear the ding - dong

Go march-in' to the ta - ble, ring.

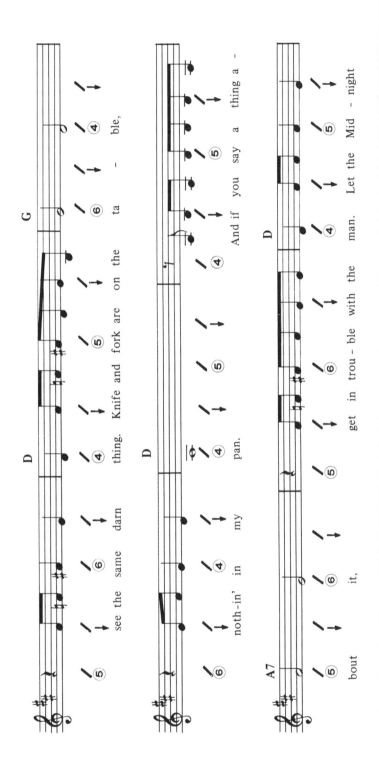

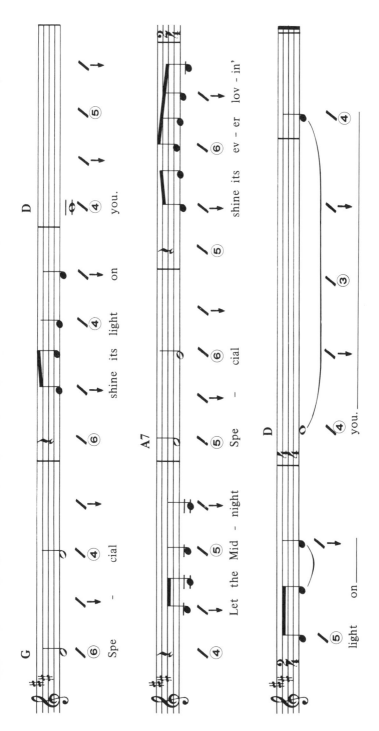

Notice that you must use different bass notes with each chord. "Frankie and Johnny" is another song that you can play in D. To *transpose* a song is to play it in a new key. Eventually, you should be able to transpose songs from one key to another with ease. The basic chords for the keys of C, E, and G are shown below.

BASIC CHORDS IN THE KEY OF C

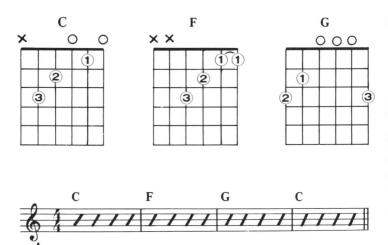

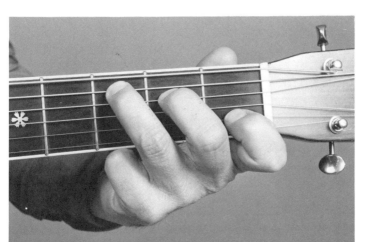

BASIC CHORDS IN THE KEY OF E

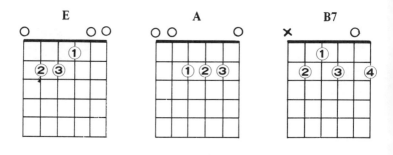

BASIC CHORDS IN THE KEY OF G

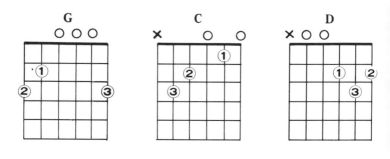

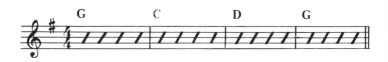

SINGLE-STRING TECHNIQUES

Everybody wants to be a lead guitarist these days—playing finger-bending solos at breakneck speed. While that is an admirable goal to strive for, we can't all be Eddie Van Halen or George Benson overnight. The best we can do is to play gracefully and tastefully—at whatever level we may be. I'd like to start your single-string playing with a series of notes that relate to a G chord. Many instructors will start you with scales or finger exercises—but that seems static and boring to me. Below, you will find a series of diagrams, each of which represents a single note. Slowly, follow these notes down until you reach the last one. Then strum a G chord. This little *riff* will get your fingers roving from the top (first) string to the bottom (sixth) string.

At first, I would recommend using a flatpick to hit these notes. Use downstrokes on each one. Later, you will want to use upstrokes (V) and downstrokes (⊓) alternately.

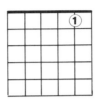

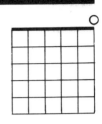

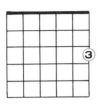

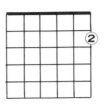

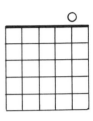

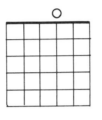

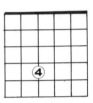

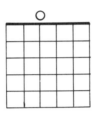

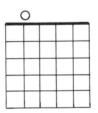

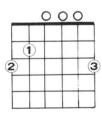

A Word About Guitar Tablature

"I think it's good to read music . . . but not neces-sarily for everybody. Ear training is really more important. I learned guitar mostly by ear."

Nancy Wilson of Heart

When reading tablature you will notice horizontal lines representing each of the strings on the guitar. The high E is on the top, and the other strings line up accordingly. Numbers placed on the lines indicate frets. The *riff* we just learned in the key of G looks like this in tablature.

Many guitarists cannot read a single note of music, and play, as they say 'by ear'. I would, however, suggest that you study musical notation at some point in your training. It can open many doors for you.

FURTHER CHORD STUDY

Mama Don't 'Low

Let's learn some more songs in different keys. To start with, let's try a bluegrass-style song called "Mama Don't 'Low." As you will see, this is the kind of song to which you can add your own verses. One of my favorite verses is: "Mama don't allow no guitar teachers around here!"

Mama Don't 'Low

E

I don't care what ma-ma don't 'low, Gon- na

A

pick my gui – tar an - y -how,

E   B7

Ma-ma don't 'low no gui-tar pick-in' 'round

E

here.

Crawdad

This next song, one of the first that I ever learned on guitar, is a natural in the key of E. Expand your strum on this song by going down (↓) and then up (↑) with the pick (or fingers). In other words, hit a bass note and then strum down/up immediately.

Crawdad

You get a line and I'll get a pole,— hon-ey.

You get a line and I'll get a pole,—

babe.   You get a line and

I'll get a pole and we'll go down to the

craw-dad hole.   Hon-ey,

ba - by mine.

Minor Chords

Try these three new chords:

A minor

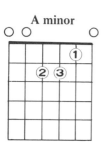

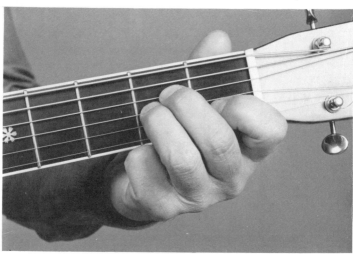

D minor

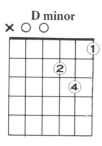

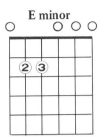

E minor

Using minor chords along with the chords you have already learned will open a whole new world of sound to you. For example:

This progression was used in countless rock and roll ballads througout the do-wop days of the 1950s. You might also want to try it in the key of G.

St. James Infirmary

Minor chords also work well in sad blues songs like this old standard, "St. James Infirmary." In a song of this type, I would suggest a slow series of rhythmic downstrokes, using your fingers or a flat-pick.

St. James Infirmary

It was down in old Joe's bar-room,— on a cor-ner by— the square.— The drinks were served-as u-sual,— and the u-su-al crowd—was there.

Now, let's put together a major and minor chord with a moving *bass run* to link them together. Starting with a G chord, hit the sixth string, strum down/up (⊓ V)—hit the sixth string at the 2nd fret (an F♯ note). Then hit the open sixth string (an E note) strumming on an E minor chord. It looks like this:

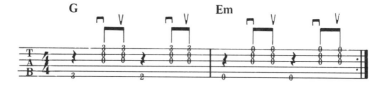

Bass runs are very important in song accompaniment and add texture to your playing. You will get to the point where you can move your right hand quickly enough to play the bass run and to reach the next chord without losing the rhythm. Remember, your touch and tone are the most important parts of your playing, at whatever level. Always pay close attention to these aspects of your playing.

FINGERPICKING:
An Introduction

Fingerpicking is perhaps the most satisfying of all guitar styles, and it is one of the most difficult to master. There are endless ways to approach this technique: from the thumping blues of Robert Johnson, Skip James, and Ry Cooder, to the subtle melodic ideas of Doc Watson, Chet Atkins, and Eric Schoenberg. Fingerpicking can be incredibly complex, but all of it rests on a simple, solid foundation.

As I mentioned before, your thumb is the pivot point of all fingerpicking. Let's start with an A chord. Slowly move your thumb back and forth from the fifth string to the fourth string. Give one beat to each note.

Now, *pinch* the fifth string and the first string, using the thumb and index finger of your right hand. Follow that by bringing your thumb down to the fourth string.

Try the same idea using an E chord:

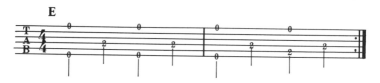

Now try a D chord:

This is the essence of fingerpicking. Later on, you may want to add your middle and ring fingers for more complex picking patterns, but for now you are well on your way. Remember to keep your thumb moving steadily in rhythm at all times.

Well, that brings us to the end of this introduction to the guitar. I hope my information has been helpful, interesting, and fun! The Bibliography will help you find books that will take you further in your study of the guitar. Don't give up! The world needs as many guitarists as it can get.

CHORD GLOSSARY

A
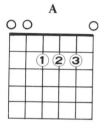

A7
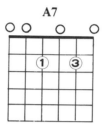

Am
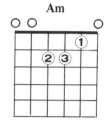

C
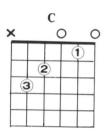

C7

Cm
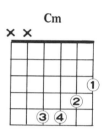

B
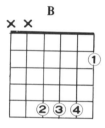

B7
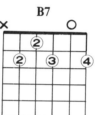

Bm
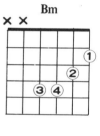

E
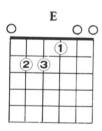

E7
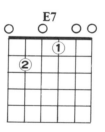

Em
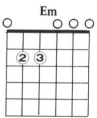

D
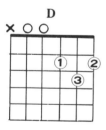

D7
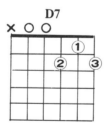

Dm
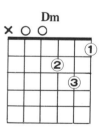

G

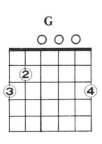

G7

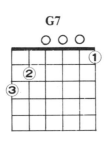

Gm

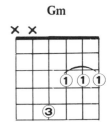

F

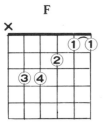

F7

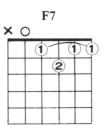

Fm

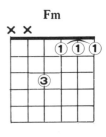

BIBLIOGRAPHY

There are many excellent resources available as you continue your study of the guitar. Here are a few ideas to try after you have learned the chords and techniques presented in this book.

Homespun Tapes (Box 694, Woodstock, New York 12498) offers a wide selection of guitar instruction on audio and video cassettes. My own series, **Rock Guitar** and **Beginning Jazz**, are available, as well as other tapes. Write for catalogue.

The Guitarist's Picture Chord Encyclopedia by John Pearse (Music Sales Corporation) features every chord a guitarist will ever need.

There are other books in Music Sales' **Picture Chords** series, including my **Jazz Picture Chords and How to Use Them.** I would recommend this to students who wish to move ahead on the guitar, whether or not they are interested in jazz.

How to Play Blues Guitar by Arlen Roth (Music Sales Corporation) offers an easygoing approach to basic chords, rhythms, and styles of the blues.

Improvising Rock Guitar by Arti Funaro and Artie Traum (Music Sales Corporation) is a more advanced study of the playing styles of Jimi Hendrix, Eric Clapton, and others.

Fingerpicking Styles for Guitar by Happy Traum (Music Sales Corporation) offers the sixteen most important fingerpicking techniques for guitar students.

There are scores of books available for guitarists, and obviously it would be impossible to list them all here. A careful glance at your local music store will reveal a world of written, taped, and filmed materials to help you progress.

Guitar Compact Reference Books

Here are other great titles in this series that you will want to add to your collection:

GUITAR

The Advanced Guitar Case Chord Book
by Askold Buk

68 pp AM 80227
ISBN 0.8256.1243.8
$4.95

Prepack AM 90176
$59.40

The Advanced Guitar Case Scale Book
by Darryl Winston

48 pp AM 91462
ISBN 0.8256.1370.1
$4.95

Prepack AM 91463
$59.40

Basic Blues Guitar
by Darryl Winston

56 pp AM 91281
ISBN 0.8256.1366.3
$4.95

Prepack AM 91246
$59.40

Beginning Guitar
by Artie Traum

64 pp AM 36997
ISBN 0.8256.2332.2
$4.95

Prepack AM 86997
$59.40

Beginning Rock Guitar
by Artie Traum

48 pp AM 37292
ISBN 0.8256.2444.4
$4.95

Prepack AM 37300
$59.40

The Compact Blues Guitar Chord Reference
compiled by Len Vogler

48 pp AM 91731
ISBN 0.8256.1385.X
$4.95

Prepack AM 91732
ISBN 0.8256.1386.8
$59.40

The Compact Rock Guitar Chord Reference
compiled by Len Vogler

48pp AM 91733
ISBN 0.8256.1387.6
$4.95

Prepack AM 91734
ISBN 0.8256.1388.4
$59.40

The Original Guitar Case Scale Book
by Peter Pickow

56 pp AM 76217
ISBN 0.8256.2588.2
$4.95

Prepack AM 86217
$59.40

Rock 'n' Roll Guitar Case Chord Book
by Russ Shipton

48 pp AM 28689
ISBN 0.86001.880.6
$4.95

Prepack AM 30891
$59.40

The Original Guitar Case Chord Book
by Peter Pickow

48 pp AM 35841
ISBN 0.8256.2998.5
$4.95

Prepack AM 36138
$59.40

Tuning Your Guitar
By Donald Brosnac

AM 35858
ISBN 0.8256.2180.1
$4.95

Prepack AM 85858
$59.40

BASS GUITAR

Beginning Bass Guitar
by Peter Pickow

80 pp AM 36989
ISBN 0.8256.2332.4
$4.95
Prepack AM 86989
$59.40

Beginning Bass Scales
by Peter Pickow

48 pp AM 87482
ISBN 0.8256.1342.6
$4.95

Prepack AM 90174
$59.40

Chord Bassics
by Jonas Hellborg

80 pp AM 60138
ISBN 0.8256.1058.3
$4.95

Prepack AM 80138
$59.40

Eight more Guitar Compact Reference Books available from Music Sales:

The Alternate Tunings Guide for Guitar
Beginning Rock Guitar
Beginning Slide Guitar
D. I. Y. Guitar Repair

Guitarist's Riff Diary
Manual de Acordes Para Guitarra
The Twelve-String Guitar Guide
Using Your Guitar

For further info contact your local music dealer or call: 914-469-2271
Music Sales Corporation • PO Box 572 • Chester, New York • 10918